Larry and Friends

Created & illustrated by Carla Torres

Written by Nat Jaspar

Design & lettering by Catalina Torres

Published by Tangerine Books 2014

First published in March 2014

ISBN: 978-1-62847-473-2

Printed in China.

LARRY

and Friends

CARLA TORRES ★ ★ ★ NAT JASPAR

It is so good to know Larry has so many friends that made this book possible.

Thank you all! ✦ 🐾

In alphabetic order: María Belén Alarcón ✦ Rosa Alarcón ✦ Gnat Atherden ✦ Steven Elliot Altman ✦ Claudia Azula Altucher ✦ Paul Baker ✦ Massie Bavarian ✦ Roxanne Bavarian ✦ Gil Beto ✦ Kaie Bird ✦ Luis Miguel Brito ✦ Myriam Bouchard ✦ Derek Brueckner Nefertiti Buckingham ✦ Valentina Camaran Dostal ✦ Alison Clarke ✦ Della Clark ✦ Xavier de la Cueva ✦ Jennifer Daffron ✦ Pilar G. Dexter ✦ Shehreyar Elahi ✦ Laura Fernández Patricia Fletcher ✦ Paulina Garcés ✦ Federico Gómez ✦ Gaspar Guerra ✦ Hernán Guerrero Saul Hudson ✦ Daniel C Jahn ✦ Kim Jones ✦ Kristin Kaineg ✦ Brian Lane Stanley ✦ Sylvia Yolande Liechti-Graber ✦ Vania Milanovitch Bastén ✦ María Caridad Moncayo ✦ Regula Neuenschwander ✦ Silvia Neves ✦ Silvia Orna ✦ Laura Osorno ✦ Amira Pérez ✦ Lake Phalgoo ✦ Donna Providenti ✦ Gabriel Roldós ✦ Maria Isabel Salvador ✦ Patricio Sarzosa Aura Sosa ✦ Isabel Sugranes ✦ Gaby Torres ✦ Margarita Torres ✦ Catalina Torres ✦ Lula Torres ✦ Marcelo Torres ✦ Merrilee Warholak ✦ Mats Wedin ✦ Steve de Weijer ✦ Atticus Wells ✦ George Winslow ✦ Stephen Winslow ✦ Pilar Zimmermann ✦ And the support of 161 other backers.

★ *To our friends from everywhere*

LARRY

the American Dog

Every day should be a happy day. At least that's what Larry the dog thinks. But today is Larry's birthday, which makes it... Double happy? Triple happy? If only he didn't have to work like a dog to get everything ready... Although Larry's a juggler, he's better at juggling balls than chores, and by mid-afternoon the house is still a mess.

But Larry doesn't care: he's very excited!

All his friends are coming! And he has so many, from all over the world. Although Larry was born in Brooklyn, living in New York has led him to befriend creatures from all over the world... each of them unique and wonderful, including one that now holds the key to his heart. Ahhhhh, he sighs, if only...

RINGADINGADONG!

The bell startles him from his reverie. His first guest has arrived! Who will it be?

Ringadingadong! Ringadingadong!

"Who is it?," asks Larry.

"Whoz alvays firzt?" says a heavily accented voice.

Larry jumps up and down. He's so glad that Magda is the first to come. The cute little pig from Poland is his partner, completing his juggling act with the most awesome tightrope stunts. She's also very good at organizing and the best person to help him finish decorating his living room for the party.

Magda was born in Kraków to very serious parents, who sent her to New York to become a competent secretary. Once Magda arrived in New York and was exposed to newer (and higher) perspectives, she came to the conclusion that if the goal was to be competent, she might as well be competent at something that she really loved. Now she is the most responsible performer in an irresponsible tightrope-walking act. As she says, "Advvventures are a fine thing, but don't forget the savvvety net or else you may fall and pfffuiiittt! You vvvecome ground meat."

Always attentive to Larry's needs, Madga has brought him a new little tie to replace his raggedy one.

Before Larry can express his thanks with a badly pronounced "dziękuję", the bell rings once more.

Ringadingadong! Ringadingadong!

Which of Larry's friends will it be now?

9

"Dziękuję" means Thank you! in Polish.

Ringadingadong! Ringadingadong!

"Who is it?," ask Larry, and Magda.

"It's meeeeeeeee," says a melodic voice. **"Heeeeeeendrik!"**

Henrik takes his time to come in. He does everything with calm, enjoying the beauty of the moment, which is not only rare because he's a hare, a species fond of speed, but because he comes from a family of highly hyperactive individuals.

While he hasn't inherited their drive, curiously he inherited their Irish accent and with it their love of ballads. He has a knack for seeing beauty even in the ugly. **Graffiti** and street grime, instead of repulsing him, have become his favorite sources of inspiration. "There is beauty in everything, you just have to open your eyes... and your heaaart."

Although he spends most of his time wandering alone through the streets in search of ideas for new poems and ballads, he's also fond of having what he calls craic, a fun time and good conversation.

And to make sure tonight will be full of it, he has composed a special song for the birthday boy: "The Ballad of Larry Boy."

Before Larry can hear it, the bell rings once more.

Ringadingadong! Ringadingadong!

Which of Larry's friends will it be now?

★ **"Graffiti"** is an art form of writing or drawings scribbled, scratched, or sprayed on a wall or other surface in a public place.

Cecilia
THE PERUVIAN LLAMA

Ringadingadong! Ringadingadong!

"Who is it?," ask Larry, Magda, and Henrik.

"Cecilia, darrrling."

Cecilia the llama is so glamorous, you would never believe her life story. She was born on the outskirts of Cuzco, Peru, and was expected to endure a life of hardship, providing the local artisans with her hair so they could fashion ponchos, sweaters, and ridiculous baby shoes.

Growing up, she saw her mother and sisters being shaved season after season. When her turn came, she thought: "¿Por qué?" Why, indeed, accept a destiny that was not hers? Warm with hair still her own, she left and never came back. She walked through mountains, jungles, and plenty of tobacco plantations until she reached New York.

Now she wears fabulous clothes (not made from llama hair) to sing in the Club Silencio. She sings of her travels, and, of course, of love. "¿Para qué todo lo demás, si no hay amor?" What good are so many things if you can't have love?

She met Larry while looking for someone to practice English with; she still speaks it "terrrribly," though she has improved greatly thanks to him. That's why she has brought him a compilation of the best **"Chicha"** music from Peru.

Before Larry can play it, the bell rings once more.

Ringadingadong! Ringadingadong!

Which of Larry's friends will it be now?

★★★

▼▼▼▼

★ **"Chicha"** is a music gender better known as Peruvian cumbia.

Gugu
THE AFRICAN ZEBRA

Ringadingadong! Ringadingadong!

"Who is it?," ask Larry, Magda, Henrik, and Cecilia.

"Your rafiki! Your bro'!" says Gugu the African zebra, who comes in chewing grass nonchalantly.

Gugu is an expert on grass. His favorite one comes from the Midwest. Its wildness reminds him of the taste of the grassy plains he grew up on in Africa.

Life is not easy for a male zebra, as Gugu discovered when he was young. There is room for only one stallion per family. Young ones have to leave and start out on their own.

Gugu decided that if he had to leave, he would go where no African zebras had gone before: New York City. With him he took his energy and his favorite **Djembe** drum. Now, years later, although he still misses his family, he has the comfort of having achieved something: he has become the lead percussionist at the Apollo Theater. "Aim high," he loves to advise his friends. "Look how well it worked for me!" Then he knocks on wood, because although he's a very optimistic zebra, he's also a slightly superstitious one.

That's why he has brought Larry an African talisman that will protect him in his journey toward wisdom and achievement.

Before Larry can put it on his wrist, the bell rings once more.

Ringadingadong! Ringadingadong!

Which of Larry's friends will it be now?

★ **"Rafiki"** means Friend in Swahili language • **"Djembe"** is a rope-tuned skin-covered goblet drum played with bare hands, originally from West Africa.

Ringadingadong! Ringadingadong!

"Who is it?," ask Larry, Magda, Henrik, Cecilia, and Gugu.

For an answer, a trumpeting sound: **"Pppprrrrrroofffff."**

It's Larry's friend Sumita the elephant. Like Larry, Sumita is a street performer. She learned the art of story-dancing—narrating stories with soft, rhythmic movements—in her native India, where she became the star of a traveling circus.

While touring in New York, Sumita took a break to visit the city and got lost in the subway. When she found her way, three days later, the circus had left her behind. She didn't cry. She knew from her stories that life sometimes takes mysterious roads to land you in the right place at the right moment. That's why she's always **bindaas**—carefree and cool.

Now you can see her perform at the Times Square station. Thanks to her, commuters slow down—if only for a few minutes—and rediscover the story of humanity.

Tonight she has brought Larry a new story-dance to give him the inspiration he needs to prepare a smashing new act.

But before Larry can watch it, the bell rings once more.

Ringadingadong! Ringadingadong!

Which of Larry's friends will it be now?

* **"Bindaas"** means Cool and Carefree (not worrying too much about anything).

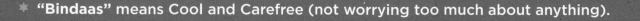

Coqui
THE PUERTORICAN FROG

Ringadingadong! Ringadingadong!

"Who is it?," ask Larry, Magda, Henrik, Cecilia, Gugu, and Sumita.

"It's me, papi."

Everybody looks surprised—who's papi?—while Larry opens the door joyfully, knowing full well that behind it stands his friend Coqui.

Everybody has to look down, for Coqui is so tiny. He came to New York from Puerto Rico as a small frog, and has not grown much bigger since. All the same, as soon as he smiles, Coqui becomes big. And when he starts to play the violin, he fills the room with sounds so wonderful that all of Larry's friends start to wiggle and twist.

The legend says that if you take a coqui frog from Puerto Rico, it will never make music again. But Coqui is the living proof that you shouldn't believe everything people say. He took one look at the moon from his pond in the Botanical Garden in the Bronx and decided it was the same sky that covered him in Puerto Rico. After all, your **casa** (or water lily) is where your heart is.

He has brought Larry—who has visited his pond more than once to listen to him—a new tune that is sure to move everybody's feet.

But before Larry can make the first one-two-three, the bell rings once more.

Ringadingadong! Ringadingadong!

Which of Larry's friends will it be now?

★ **"Papi"** means Daddy in Spanish • **"Casa"** means House in Spanish.

Ringadingadong! Ringadingadong!

"Who is it?," ask Larry, Magda, Henrik, Cecilia, Gugu, Sumita, and Coqui.

"Ni hao," says Fu the Chinese dragon.

Larry salutes Fu with a high five... or should we say high three, because, like any dragon unrelated to a Chinese emperor, Fu only has three fingers per paw instead of the royal five.

But that is no impediment for him to be one of the best massage therapists in the city. In his Chinatown office, he has fixed the muscles of thousands of backs and necks so people can feel **hao hao**, or good good, once more.

His father, who was born in Beijing and immigrated to New York before Fu was born, taught him everything about acupuncture, and also explained to him that most people get sick from fear. "Fear—especially fear of change—is your own worst enemy, my son," he used to caution Fu in his native Mandarin. "And what is life, after all, but change?"

So that Larry can benefit from change instead of fearing it, Fu has brought him a very special Chinese book, the **I Ching**, which will give Larry the guidance he needs. Fu reads it often, but has to be very careful while doing it: he has burned over a dozen copies with his fiery sneezes!

Before Larry can thank him with a heartfelt **"xie xie,"** the bell rings once more.

Ringadingadong! Ringadingadong!

Which of Larry's friends will it be now?

★ **"Ni hao"** means Hi! in Chinese • **"Xie xie"** means Thank you! in Chinese
"I Ching" is an ancient Chinese manual of divination (oracle).

Ringadingadong! Ringadingadong!

"Who is it?," ask Larry, Magda, Henrik, Cecilia, Gugu, Sumita, Coquí, and Fu.

Silence.

Ringadingadong! Ringadingadong!

Curious, Larry opens the door to find... no one!

At the third **'ringadingadong,'** Larry finally gets it. It's the telephone! He rushes to answer it. It's his friend Pedrito, the Ecuadorian guinea pig, calling from London, where he's touring with his band QuitoPeroNoPongo.

For many years, Pedrito could not travel internationally because his father made a mistake in the immigration forms when the family moved to the US, leaving the poor guinea pig without papers.

There were only two options left: to cry or to laugh. Pedrito decided to laugh, which was made easier by what they call the **'sal quiteña,'** a very special sense of humor typical from his country. And in those days when his lack of papers was able to rob him of his sense of humor, he would hit his drums until he was able to smile again. His talent with this instrument, a taste for using it as a sort of surfing table to go over the audience, and his contagious joy have made of him one of the most famous rocks stars of the decade.

Imagine the happiness of his band mates and fans in the whole world, when Pedrito finally was able to travel.

For Larry, the phone call in itself is the best gift—it reminds him that no matter the distance, they will always remain close friends.

But before he can share this thought with Pedrito, the bell rings once more.

Ringadingadong! Ringadingadong!

Which of Larry's friends will it be now?

★ **"Sal quiteña"** is a special sense of humor typical of the people from Quito.

Bernard
THE FRENCH GARGOYLE

Ringadingadong! Ringadingadong!

"Who is it?," ask Larry, Magda, Henrik, Cecilia, Gugu, Sumita, Coqui, and Fu.

"Berrrnarrrrd, the gargoyle."

Larry met Bernard one day on the street and was so enchanted by the 1,001 stories told by the French gargoyle that they became fast friends.

Bernard knows everything about people—he spent years observing them from his cozy place on the roof of the Notre-Dame Cathedral in Paris. Seeing so many tourists made him very curious about other cultures, so he decided to pack his belongings, travel the world, and, **voilà**, he ended up in New York.

Bernard knows that all knowledge is worthless unless it's shared. That's why he has brought Larry one of his most beloved possessions: a beautiful map for Larry to use to plan a trip around the world and experience the wonders of other cultures.

"But therrr izzzz morrrr," says Bernard with his guttural accent. "I have also brought you the subway pass!" For isn't New York a small replica of the world? Each neighborhood a country, each borough a continent? Not a bad start at all!

Before Larry can say **"Oh là là!,"** the bell rings once more.

Ringadingadong! Ringadingadong!

Which of Larry's friends will it be now?

★ **"Voilà"** means That's it! in French • **"Oh là là"** means Oh dear! in French.

Rimshi
THE TIBETAN YAK

Ringadingadong! Ringadingadong!

"Who is it?," ask Larry, Magda, Henrik, Cecilia, Gugu, Sumita, Coqui, Fu, and Bernard.

"Namaste, friend Larry," says a peaceful voice. **"It's Rimshi."**

Rimshi the yak hails from Tibet, a country that she was forced to leave because of an invasion by the Chinese. Life as a refugee has not been easy. No home, no family, not even a familiar sight to warm her heart. But hardship has made Rimshi stronger and she knows that where there is adversity there is also opportunity.

That's why she always keeps a bag full of dreams... some of them have come true already, others may in the future. It's just a matter of patience.

Larry met Rimshi when volunteering at the refugee center where she works. A fulfilling friendship was born based on their shared desire to make the world a better place as well as their love of music, for Rimshi enjoys singing and playing the guitar in her free time.

For his birthday, she has brought Larry a very special Tibetan banner to bring peace into his home.

Before Larry can say **"Namaste,"** the bell rings once more.

Ringadingadong! Ringadingadong!

Which of Larry's friends will it be now?

★ **"Namaste"** is a powerful form of salutation that means "The Light within me recognizes and honors the Light within you".

27

Ringadingadong! Ringadingadong!

"Who is it?," ask Larry, Magda, Henrik, Cecilia, Gugu, Sumita, Coqui, Fu, Bernard, and Rimshi.

"Cheecheecheechee," comes the sound of maracas.

It's Oscar the Dominican sea urchin, who will insist they all dance a merengue. It took Larry years to learn not to step on his partner while dancing it.

Oscar is a musician. He has been playing maracas since he was old enough to hold a pacifier. It was "cheecheecheechee," from morning to night. The sound would have driven any parent nuts, but his mom had Dominican rhythm dancing through her blood and found it rather cheery.

Oscar is the leader of the band Oscar Erizo y sus Players, which was born in Washington Heights but is now famous through the whole country with the hit "Hasta la Vista No Way!" But Oscar doesn't care about success. He's just following the voice inside his head that says, "Shake it, baby, shake it." He knows happiness is contagious, like music, so he wants to add his granito de sal or grain of salt. "Life is all about **sabor**—you know, flavor."

For Larry's birthday, he has brought a shell that allows you to hear the sound of the Caribbean when you put it next to your ear.

Before Larry can say **"gracias,"** the bell rings once more.

Ringadingadong! Ringadingadong!

Which of Larry's friends will it be now?

★ **"Gracias"** means Thank you! in Spanish • **"Sabor"** means Flavor in Spanish.

Ringadingadong! Ringadingadong!

"Who is it?," ask Larry, Magda, Henrik, Cecilia, Gugu, Sumita, Coqui, Fu, Bernard, Rimshi, and Oscar.

"It's Jin, open the door, my dear friends!"

Larry adores Jin the fox, although sometimes he has a hard time understanding her accent, which transforms Rs into softer Ls as if by magic—for sweet Jin comes all the way from Korea.

Larry and Jin need no words to understand each other. It took Larry one look at Jin's paintings to realize that they were meant to be friends. Everything Jin learned about painting—and that is a lot—she taught herself. She failed more than once at the beginning, but through perseverance, she achieved the most amazing works of art. As Jin often says, "Plactice makes pelfect."

When she reached a point where her art would not grow unless her mind grew as well, Jin left Korea and came to live with some relatives in Flushing, New York. There, the variety and the chaos make her soul—and her painting—grow richer by the hour.

She gives Larry a teeny-tiny painting as a gift; but in it is all of her very big heart.

Before Larry can thank her, the bell rings once more.

Ringadingadong! Ringadingadong!

Which of Larry's friends will it be now?

Ringadingadong! Ringadingadong!

"Who is it?," ask Larry, Magda, Henrik, Cecilia, Gugu, Sumita, Coqui, Fu, Bernard, Rimshi, Oscar, and Jin.

"Sono iiiiioooooooooooooooo," answers Fabio in the singing Italian he favors over plain English.

A simple "It's me" doesn't sound dramatic, and drama—imaginary or real—is what Fabio lives for. He blames it on his Italian descent, but everybody knows Fabio is the only drama king in a family of very hardworking and slightly pushy rams.

Although his family lives in Little Italy, Fabio moved uptown to be closer to the opera, where he performs daily. There he plays truants, devils, and deceiving lovers.

Often the characters remain with him offstage and he starts acting like a diva. When that happens he knows it's time to visit his 103-year-old great-grandmother, who inspired him to become a singer with her lullabies. **"Caro,** priiide is a daaaangerous thing," she always reminds him. "It sneakssss in without you knowing it and takes awaaaay what you love the mossst."

The same great-grandmother helped him prepare a delicious lasagna, which he has brought as a birthday treat.

Before Larry can thank him with a sonorous **"grazie"**, the bell rings once more.

Ringadingadong! Ringadingadong!

Which of Larry's friends will it be now?

✳ **"Sono io"** means It's me! in Italian • **"Caro"** means Darling! in Italian
"Grazie" means Thank you! in Italian.

Rosita
THE MEXICAN COYOTE

Ringadingadong! Ringadingadong!

"Who is it?," ask Larry, Magda, Henrik, Cecilia, Gugu, Sumita, Coqui, Fu, Bernard, Rimshi, Oscar, Jin, and Fabio.

"Your Destiny," says a playful, girlish voice.

Larry's heart beats faster. He has such a crush on Rosita, the Mexican coyote! And now here she is, calling herself his destiny. If only! Blushing, he ushers her into the house.

Rosita doesn't notice. She's rather fond of Larry although she hides it better than he does, for she's very strong. Not only did she survive the tough trip from Mexico guided by some chicken people that dared to call themselves coyotes, she's now the best luchadora in New York. Those who fight La Primorosa—as she's called—know that she's invincible. "When you believe you will win, you win. **Órale!** It's that simple."

She's applying the same theory to catch Larry but—to her disappointment—results have been slow. Larry is shyer than Mexican dogs are, especially shyer than the escuincles, the hairless ones. They are so fast and descarados, they scare girls away!

That's why, after wondering for days what to bring Larry—a mole dish from her native town of Oaxaca?—she has decided to give him a little kiss, a besito.

Before Larry can receive this gift from her pouty lips, the bell rings once more.

Ringadingadong! Ringadingadong!

Which of Larry's friends will it be now?

★ **"Órale"** means Let's go! in Mexican slang.

Ringadingadong! Ringadingadong!

"Who is it?," ask Larry, Magda, Henrik, Cecilia, Gugu, Sumita, Coqui, Fu, Bernard, Rimshi, Oscar, Jin, Fabio, and Rosita.

"Ulises!!!"

Larry cannot believe that Ulises has arrived so early, given his friend's propensity for losing his way.

You would think that Ulises would know his way around, since he was born in New York. But his Greek roots made him choose Astoria as his neighborhood and he seldom leaves the few blocks that surround his restaurant, Ulises' Soul Food.

Ulises is a cook. Although he specializes in Greek specialties like **spanakopita**—a spinach pie that has become Larry's favorite dish—he also cooks recipes from other countries. The only non-negotiable condition is that it has to make you feel warm inside. As he says, "Good food feeds not only the stomach but the soul."

For once, Ulises has not brought spanakopita as a gift, but Larry is not disappointed, because next to Ulises is the biggest and most beautiful birthday cake he has ever seen.

But before Larry can say "efcharistó", the bell rings once more.

Ringadingadong! Ringadingadong!

Which of Larry's friends will it be now?

37

★ **"Efcharistó"** means Thank you! in Greek • **"Spanakopita"** is a Greek spinach pie.

Laila
THE IRANIAN CAT

Ringadingadong! Ringadingadong!

"Who is it?," ask Larry, Magda, Henrik, Cecilia, Gugu, Sumita, Coqui, Fu, Bernard, Rimshi, Oscar, Jin, Fabio, Rosita, and Ulises.

"Laila," silkily announces a beautiful, sinewy cat.

When Laila enters the room, it seems she's floating instead of walking on her delicate paws. Everybody stares at her, but Laila doesn't mind, she's used to it. She's been stared at since she was a tiny kitten.

In her native Iran, people stared at her because of her eyes (slightly too intense). Or because of the hijab she used to cover her head (always slightly off center). Or because of her being an entomologist—after all, most cats are supposed to hunt insects, not study them.

Tired of always feeling slightly out of place, she accepted an offer to work at the American Museum of Natural History in New York. She thought that in a city so huge she would certainly get lost in the crowd. But again people stared at her—this time because of her grace and beauty. With time, Laila has learned to accept this fact. The important thing is always to be yourself, no matter who stares at you.

To lead Larry in the search for himself, she has brought him a jar filled with beautiful fireflies.

Before Larry can thank her with the only Farsi word he knows, **"Tashakkur"**, the bell rings once more.

Ringadingadong! Ringadingadong!

Which of Larry's friends will it be now?

39

★ **"Tashakkur"** means Thank you! in Farsi, one of the languages spoken in Iran.

Ashki
THE NATIVE AMERICAN BUFFALO

Ringadingadong! Ringadingadong!

"Who is it?," ask Larry, Magda, Henrik, Cecilia, Gugu, Sumita, Coqui, Fu, Bernard, Rimshi, Oscar, Jin, Fabio, Rosita, and Laila.

"Ashki," says a very deep and sedate voice.

Larry is surprised. He didn't expect Ashki, the Native American buffalo, to come. Ashki is seldom in New York. His work as a shaman takes him all over the country to help people clear spirits that haunt them.

Ashki was trained by his father, who was trained by his father, and so on, in a tradition that has endured for several hundred years. His magic is inspired by nature—from the sky to the lakes, from the tiniest of plants to the biggest of animals.

"The world around us is alive," he often tells people who ask for his help. "It talks to us and would gladly give us the answer to our questions if only we would listen."

Every time he's in New York, Ashki enjoys Larry's company. The dog's antics give him the joy he needs to cope with a city of iron and concrete, where plants (and illusions) are scarce.

Ashki has few earthly possessions besides his wisdom, so for a birthday present he's giving Larry one of the precious feathers from his headdress.

Before Larry can thank him, the bell rings once more.

Ringadingadong! Ringadingadong!

Which of Larry's friends will it be now?

41

Edgar
THE COLOMBIAN CAIMAN

Ringadingadong! Ringadingadong!

"Who is it?," ask Larry, Magda, Henrik, Cecilia, Gugu, Sumita, Coqui, Fu, Bernard, Rimshi, Oscar, Jin, Fabio, Rosita, Ulises, Laila, and Ashki.

"The Gator, Larry," says a raspy voice.

Edgar's nickname, Gator, has become so popular with his friends that only a few remember his real name. Larry is one of them.

He met Edgar a few days after the Gator came to New York from Colombia. Edgar was playing the accordion on a street corner to make enough money to rent a room.

Larry asked why Edgar left Colombia for this. Edgar, looking at his accordion with love, said, "Nobody is a prophet in his own land, especially when it comes to the accordion. Here I can finally find the audience I wanted." Admiring his answer, Larry decided to become his friend and help him.

Edgar now lives with a Colombian family in Jackson Heights, and has a steady gig playing traditional accordion tunes at a French restaurant in Manhattan. He is also experimenting with popular Latin songs such as "Se va el **Caimán**," as well as American ones like "See You Later, Alligator." To make sure Larry is wide awake to enjoy his party, the Gator has brought him one pound of exquisite Colombian coffee.

Before Larry can take a sip, the bell rings once more.

Ringadingadong! Ringadingadong!

Which of Larry's friends will it be now?

★ **"Caiman"** is a small crocodile that lives in Central and South America.

Katsuo
THE JAPANESE MONKEY

Ringadingadong! Ringadingadong!

"Who is it?," ask Larry, Magda, Henrik, Cecilia, Gugu, Sumita, Coqui, Fu, Bernard, Rimshi, Oscar, Jin, Fabio, Rosita, Ulises, Laila, Ashki, and Edgar.

"Konnichiwa, Larry-san," Katsuo, the Japanese monkey, salutes him.

As Larry opens the door, a flash blinds him. Katsuo is fond of photography and never stops snapping shots.

He has taken thousands of photographs of Larry, whom he met years ago in the judo class he teaches. At the time, Larry was small and tired of being bullied. Katsuo showed him how to defend himself using his opponent's strength. Katsuo is a pacifist—coming from a family that suffered much during the Second World War—but he believes peace comes from respect and clear limits. "When you let yourself be put down, the balance is broken."

Katsuo has been here so long he calls himself a New Yorker, yet sometimes he still feels homesick. When this happens, he goes to a sushi restaurant and feels better. Good thing that there is hardly a block in the city without one!

He has brought Larry a camera he ordered especially from Japan, with an extra-long-lasting battery and a gigantic memory card, so he can take hundreds of pictures.

Before Larry can test it, the bell rings once more.

Ringadingadong! Ringadingadong!

Which of Larry's friends will it be now?

★ **"Konnichiwa, Larry-san"** means Hello Mr. Larry! in Japanese.

Igor
THE RUSSIAN BEAR

Ringadingadong! Ringadingadong!

"Who is it?," ask Larry, Magda, Henrik, Cecilia, Gugu, Sumita, Coqui, Fu, Bernard, Rimshi, Oscar, Jin, Fabio, Rosita, Ulises, Laila, Ashki, Edgar, and Katsuo.

"Privet," grunts Igor the bear in his native Russian.

Although Igor arrived in New York when he was very young, living in Brighton Beach—the center of the Russian community—has kept him in touch with his language and culture.

When he spends the whole day with his family, he even forgets where he is. And it is not until the evening comes and he goes to Coney Island to perform his magic tricks that he remembers he is in New York, or, as his grandfather the intellectual used to call it, the city of peace.

"You have the chance to live in a place where tolerance is the rule and everyone is welcome," his grandpa said. "Don't take it for granted. Be grateful every day."

Every time Igor asks a person to pick a card for his most popular trick and the person answers with a new accent or language, the feeling of wonder and gratefulness instilled by his grandpa returns and fills him with immense happiness.

To remember that there is always more to life than meets the eye, Igor has brought a set of nesting dolls in the shape of a dog that looks pretty much like Larry himself.

Before Larry can play with it, the light goes suddenly off.

It is time for...

★ **"Privet"** means Hello! in Russian.

Singing "Happy Birthday"... in every language!

HAPPY BIRTHDAY!

"Larry—we wish you many more to come."

And now it's time to leave everybody to enjoy themselves, dancing, eating, and celebrating in what has become the best birthday party ever!

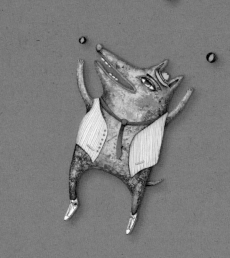

✳ the End ✳

Carla Torres is an illustrator born and raised in Ecuador. In 2005 she landed in New York looking to expand her mind, her soul, and her vision as an artist. Since then her work has been exhibited in several venues locally and internationally and has won several illustration awards. She has illustrated many children's books, Larry and Friends is her first book as an author and illustrator.

www.carlatorres.com

Nat Jaspar is a writer. She was born in Belgium, grew up in Venezuela, and moved to New York in 1997—the first place where she finally felt like she belonged. She has worked as a journalist, a copywriter, and an editor. She's obsessed with blogs and her short stories have appeared in Spanish-language literary sites.

She started writing children's stories for her niece a few years ago and got hooked from then on. She loves all characters from Larry and Friends, but if you push her to choose and push and push... she will finally confess that Cecilia, the Peruvian llama who challenges her fate, is her favorite one.

facebook.com/natjaspar